more **readers**
reading more

more
readers

reading more

publishers and libraries working together to expand the market for books

First published in 2006 by
The Reading Agency
P.O. Box 96
St Albans
Hertfordshire
AL1 3WP
www.readingagency.org.uk

Reading Partners have received an investment
from Arts & Business New Partners to develop
their creative partnership. Arts & Business New Partners
is funded by Arts Council England and the Department
for Culture, Media and Sport.

Author: Tom Palmer
Editorial Support: Katie Bond, Jane Mathieson
and Ruth Wells
Cover Design: Lee Motley
Interior Design: Terence Caven
Production: Tiina Wastie

Printed in Italy by Graphicom srl.

how to **use this book**

more readers reading more is a handbook for library reader development workers and publishers.

It has three main IDEAS sections focusing on The Reader, Author Events and Book Promotions, followed by three INFORMATION sections about Libraries, Publishers and General Information.

www.readingagency.org.uk/reading_partners holds further information, including more detailed reports and regularly updated contact lists and databases.

page 9
INTRODUCTIONS. Preface. Who is this book for? Why should libraries and publishers work together? What is Reading Partners? What libraries and publishers have learned by working together. Some quick statistics about libraries.

IDEAS
page 19
THE READER. On reading groups. Who uses them? What do they read? Who are library users? How do you create word of mouth? Great projects promoting backlist, new literary titles, poetry and new writers.

On book covers. Using proof copies to build a readership. How can you improve disabled access to reading groups?

page 51
AUTHOR EVENTS. Authors on library events. How to promote and run events. Why have events? Readers' Days. Events with new writers. Events to support book promotions. Local authors for local libraries. Young readers.

page 79
BOOK PROMOTIONS. How to promote emerging writers. Can you encourage non-poetry readers to read poetry? How to get men to read more and join libraries. Zoning fiction and non-fiction – changing book display. Book acquisition in libraries.

INFORMATION

page 91
LIBRARIES. How are libraries changing? Where are libraries? Who should publishers contact and how? What do libraries do? Transport to each region of the UK. Regional reader development networks.

page 121

PUBLISHERS. Publisher and publicity contacts. How to pitch to publishers. Library specialists at publishers.

page 132

GENERAL INFORMATION. Databases. The best library venues. Where authors live. What publishers have to offer libraries. What libraries have to offer publishers over the next calendar year. The library-publisher-supplier code of practice.

preface

This book comes from Reading Partners, an exciting
new alliance of publishers and libraries.

We're passionate about libraries and the way they
connect millions of people to the world of reading.
There's real potential for them to become buzzing
21st century community hubs for reading.

Together, led by The Reading Agency, we've spent
the last two years in an experimental pilot, exploring how
adult publishers and libraries can work together better to
achieve this. This book is about passing on and building
on all we've learnt. You can read about our new research,
about the skills librarians and publishers are learning from
each other, about how to tap into the powerful network of
library reading groups...and an awful lot more.

It's fantastic to be forging ahead with building new
working relationships with profound implications for
readers. And we're really grateful to Arts & Business,
Arts Council Scotland and MLA for being our funding
partners.

Amanda Ridout, Harper Collins, on behalf of the
Reading Partners publishers

Miranda McKearney, The Reading Agency

who is this book for?

more readers reading more is for publishers interested in expanding the market for their books – and for library workers interested in creating a vibrant reading service through reader development.

Expanding the market. Growing the market. Reader development. These phrases – whether commercially or socially motivated – all mean the same thing. More readers being inspired to read more books.

This book hopes to help answer some questions. How do you find readers for a first time novelist? Where do you find books for a first time reader? Which libraries run the best book festivals and events? Which publishers are most open to working with libraries? How can publishers and libraries work together on promotions?

Using short case studies about Reading Partners projects and advice from libraries and publishers, this book will stimulate inspiration, ideas and cooperation between two sectors who are trying to achieve some of the same ends.

Throughout *more readers reading more* you can refer to www.readingagency.org.uk/reading_partners for further information, case studies and regularly updated contact lists.

Tom Palmer

why should **libraries** and **publishers** work **together**?

- to create new readers
- to encourage established readers to read more widely
- so that publishers can learn from libraries' contact with millions of readers
- so libraries can learn marketing and publicity skills to help live literature challenge other live arts
- because publishers have authors, books and publicity machines to support library activities
- because libraries have the readers, event venues and spaces to showcase books
- because both librarians' and publishers' main reasons for doing the job they do is that they love reading and want to share their love of books with other people
- to strengthen libraries' promotion of backlist and range
- to create new audiences for live literature
- to help make sure the UK book world remains broad and innovative

what is **Reading Partners**?

Reading Partners was set up in April 2004 to explore ways that libraries and publishers can cooperate.

The Reading Agency brought together senior publishers from the nine leading London houses and a library worker from each of the home nations and England's nine regions to steer the project. Hundreds more librarians and publishers took part.

In its first two years Reading Partners piloted dozens of models of author events, book promotions and ways of working with reading groups.

It managed databases to allow publishers and libraries to cooperate more widely and more immediately.

It worked with a sample of 48 reading groups from across the UK to make sure readers' voices were heard.

It also carried out research, helped develop book supply from publishers to libraries, and trialed innovative new models of libraries working with communities.

Reading Partners attracted investment from Arts & Business allowing for a major skill sharing programme and the publication of this book. It also gained further funding to allow it to take this work forward after its initial two year pilot.

what libraries and publishers have learned from two years of working together

'Reading Partners has illustrated that there's more to publishing than just selling. The libraries play a vital role supporting publishing by enabling the public to have access to the wealth of titles in print.'
Andrew Belshaw, Pan MacMillan sales rep

'Reading Partners has defiantly broken down barriers. Publishers are more approachable. We know who to contact, where and how to grab their attention.'
Ruth Wells, South East Libraries Reader Development Coordinator

'It's become clear to me how the libraries are pivotal to their communities. Not just through their contact with the book borrowers, but also through supporting reading groups, local community groups, their links with schools and generally having their finger on the community pulse.'
Helen Johnstone, Publicity Manager, HarperCollins Fiction

'Reading Partners has raised the profile of libraries. Publishers now recognise the role libraries have in the promotion of books and authors, as well as the unique contact and dialogue libraries have with their readers.'
Nicola Thomas, Solihull Libraries

'It's been a great opportunity to share our enthusiasm and commitment to working with readers and to know that the publishers value our skills and experience.'
Lynn Hodgkins, East Midlands Libraries

'Working with the library sector offers publishers a new way of marketing books. It enables us to reach directly into a dedicated reading community, to a ready-made audience of book lovers to whom we've not spoken before. We've discovered (and it seems so obvious now!) that not only are these readers receptive to our wonderful books, but they are also happy to be seduced by the new, fresh voices at work today. Although loyal to established writers, library borrowers are also willing to try the unfamiliar and experiment with a vast range of great writing.'
Joanna Prior, Penguin Books

some **quick statistics**

- 22% of borrowers have liked a borrowed book so much they have bought it

- 36% of borrowers say they have discovered a new author by borrowing a book from the library

- 40% of readers obtain the books they read from public libraries

- 55% of borrowers also buy books some of the time

- 70% of the Great Britain's heaviest readers have a library card

- There are 4,204 libraries in the UK*

These statistics were drawn from BML's Book Reading and Library Use 2005 *research. Except * which was drawn from* CIFPA Public Library statistics 2004-2005.

the reader

interview with **anne tucker**, library **reading group member**

Questions from publishers' publicists and library reader development workers

How does your group choose its books?

The library runs a poll. Each of us suggests two books we'd like to read. Then we vote for a top 10. The library provides a set of books.

It's raining, you're busy, you've not finished the book. You still go to the library. Why?

Because people who use the library have such different experiences, opinions and attitudes. I often come out of the meetings with a new perspective on a book or a novelist.

Do you ever pretend to have read a book at the reading group?

Never. It does happen that one or more members hasn't read the book - or, more frequently, hasn't finished it (myself included) - but nobody hides that.

What book have you read that you thought you'd hate, but ended up loving?

I'm not very interested in some authors – because of a preconception that I won't like them. Beryl Bainbridge, for example. I'd never have read a book by her if it hadn't been on the list.

How much do you spend on books a year?

£250

Do you buy books by authors you've discovered at reading groups?

Yes.

What influences your choice of a book - reviews, advertising, book displays in libraries and shops or a personal recommendation?

All of these – except advertising.

Do you always read to the end of a book?

I stop reading if I *really* don't like a book. I haven't time to read books that do nothing for me. It's not a course syllabus – it's a reading group.

the library reading group top ten books 2005*

1. *The Time Traveller's Wife* – Audrey Niffenegger

2. *The Bookseller of Kabul* – Anne Seirstad

3. *Star of the Sea* – Joseph O'Connor

4. *No 1 Ladies Detective Agency* – Alexander McCall Smith

5. *A Long Way Down* – Nick Hornby

6. *The Lovely Bones* – Alice Sebold

7. *Toast* – Nigel Slater

8. *Shadow of the Wind* – Carlos Ruiz Zafon

9. *To Kill a Mockingbird* – Harper Lee

10. *The Colour* – Rose Tremain

* – email survey carried out on a sample of 48 reading groups who supported Reading Partners during 2004 and 2005

library **reading groups** – some **facts**

It is estimated that public libraries support around 4,500 reading groups with a range of services including group leaders, multiple copies of books and events. Libraries also offer advice on where to find reading groups or how to set one up.*

There are reading groups for adults, black readers, children, teenagers, families, gay and lesbian readers, the visually impaired, amongst many others.

The Reading Agency manages a growing database of over 1000 groups, searchable by postcode or type of group – www.readinggroups.peoplesnetwork.gov.uk.

50% of adults in library reading groups say they read more books as a result of being in the group. 45% say they borrow more books. 17% say they buy more books.**

* First stage mapping exercise as part of National Library
Development Programme for Reading Groups, TRA 2005
** Reading Groups and Public Library research, Book Marketing
Limited and the Reading Partnership, 2000

how libraries create word of mouth

One: Library staff are passionate about books. They talk to library users about them. They know their stuff. They know their readers. 'Try this novel.' 'I've saved a book for you.' 'I thought you might like this.'

Two: There are 4,204 libraries in the UK. Each has between one and fifty ever-changing book displays.

Three: If a library reading group chooses a book, between 10 and 25 people will read it and talk about it that night. If each of these people tells just four friends about the book, that's 40 to 100 people who know about it from just one group reading it.

Four: On websites, newsletters and notice boards, librarians produce thousands of column inches about books that help millions of readers to connect to each other, share reading tips and join in book chains.

Five: Libraries promote author events in dozens of ways. Thousands of people hear about the author and the book, whether they attend the event or not.

choosing tomorrow's classics

Vintage working with reading groups throughout the UK

For years librarians have been talking to their readers, involving them in decisions.

Recognising this, Vintage wanted to work with libraries to find out what readers think of their books.

They asked 48 library reading groups to choose the books for an important promotion: Which 15 books – from a list of 100 recognised modern classics of today – would be classics in a century's time?

The groups took up the challenge. They read all 100 books. They debated. They met once a week instead of once a month. They put aside their likes and dislikes to say 'This will be a classic' or 'This is just a flash in the pan.' They faced their task with responsibility. The 15 books they chose were:

All Quiet on the Western Front – Erich Maria
      Remarque
Atonement – Ian McEwan
Birdsong – Sebastian Faulks
Brave New World – Aldous Huxley
Captain Corelli's Mandolin – Louis de Bernieres

Catch-22 – Joseph Heller
The Curious Incident of the Dog in the Night-Time –
     Mark Haddon
The French Lieutenant's Woman – John Fowles
The Handmaid's Tale – Margaret Atwood
To Kill a Mockingbird - Harper Lee
Memoirs of a Geisha – Arthur Golden
The Name of the Rose – Umberto Eco
One Day in the Life of Ivan Denisovich – Alexander
     Solzhenitsyn
Star of the Sea – Joseph O'Connor
The Time Traveller's Wife – Audrey Niffenegger

Vintage created a promotion to showcase the fifteen books chosen. There were enough posters, stickers and postcards for each of the UK's 4,204 libraries.

Vintage also ran the promotion in the national media and in bookstores. The posters read:

To celebrate our fifteenth birthday Vintage asked forty-eight reading groups affiliated to libraries around the UK to help select fifteen of its books that will still be read in 100 years' time.

To say thank you, Vintage gave each library a set of 100 books and each of the 750 reading group members the top 15 books.

The debate hit national radio and newspapers.

The reading groups asked if they could read more of the long list at future meetings.

Many readers said that, because of *their* involvement, they'd read books they'd always wanted to read, but had never got round to. And many others said they never thought they'd read these kinds of books – but that they loved them.

> For a full report on this project see:
> www.readingagency.org.uk/reading_partners
>
> And for more information:
> www.vintagefutureclassics.co.uk

———————— ✳ ————————

"

The group were very
honoured that they had been
chosen to participate in the
Reading Partners project...
all members are of African-
Caribbean origin and most of
the time read books by black
authors. This gave then the
opportunity to read
something different – i.e.
modern classics – and they
thoroughly enjoyed the
experience.

Britta Heyworth
Reader Development Librarian, Leeds Libraries

"

judge a book by its cover

Time Warner with reading groups in Camberley and Manchester

Library reading groups don't only talk about a book's story – they talk about the author, the blurb on the back, how a book made them feel. Often groups talk about a cover and if it fits the book.

Time Warner wanted to know why some of their best authors' books weren't selling as well as they should. Was it the covers?

They gave readers in two library reading groups six books each. The readers filled in questionnaires about the cover images, blurbs and uses of quotes.

Then they were allowed to read the books.

Time Warner took a jacket designer, a blurb writer and a publicist to meet the groups. Did the groups like the covers? Did the books match up to the readers' expectations after seeing the covers?

The groups loved some covers and hated others.

One reader liked what another reader loathed. Every reader is different.

Most readers read endorsement quotes.

Some doubted them.

All were impressed by the mention of a book prize.

They thought spine design was important.

They liked books that were branded as part of a series.

They liked embossed and debossed.

They didn't like big gold lettering.

Time Warner showed the groups the new cover designs for Anita Shreve's books. A shift from scenes without people to close ups of faces, hands or eyes.

Did the groups prefer the new ones?

Most did. They like people on covers. It draws them into the story. Makes it more human.

Reading groups can be candid. They don't gush. They're real readers. Some of the things they said were blunt – if you consider the designer and blurb writer were in the room.

But the readers learned that there's a lot more to producing a cover than whim. They talked face to face with publishers. They shared ideas.

'In spite of the harsh criticism,' said a publisher. 'I thought it refreshing to hear readers' views expressed with such honesty.'

At their next meeting the reading group said how enthused they had been by meeting the publishers – the insight it had given them into what goes on in a publishing house.

Time Warner must have enjoyed the candour.

It gave them ideas for changes they could make to how they put covers together.

And they wanted more.

The next year they approached six reading groups – from the Shetlands down to Kent – and asked them to help design the cover of a first novel. From scratch.

'I now feel that publishers and libraries are on the same side,' said a librarian who runs one of the two groups. 'Which has made planning events and communicating with publishers so much easier.'

> For a full report on this project see:
> www.readingagency.org.uk/reading_partners

---— ✳ ——---

book of the **month**

A Penguin promotion throughout the UK

Libraries love quality promotional material. Posters showcasing novels that will inspire book lovers to take their reading in new directions. And more.

In the past, libraries have struggled to get their hands on quality publicity material from publishers without 'Available at all good bookshops' written all over it.

Launching their *Readers' Book of the Month*, Penguin committed to supplying each of the UK's libraries with as many bespoke posters, flyers, shelf talkers and stickers as they needed. Quality material that they ran by a panel of librarians before going to print.

The idea behind the promotion was to offer a book a month that library reading groups and other library users might be interested in. Penguin worked with librarians to choose each month's book, using quotes from real readers on the flyers.

It worked.

Displays in libraries attracted readers. Many joined reading groups as a result. Reading groups chose the books to read at future meetings.

Penguin said 'The library staff were without exception very enthusiastic – organised, efficient and very capable.'

Penguin wanted to make their *Readers' Book of the Month* an annual promotion. They ran it again. With more time for planning, they approached 12 reading groups – one in each of the UK's regions. They asked them to choose 6 books. The groups chose:

Things Fall Apart – Chinua Achebe
A Short History of Tractors in Ukrainian – Marina Lewycka
The Great Stink – Clare Clarke
The Day of Light – Graham Swift
Jacob's Gift – Jonathan Freedland
The Accidental – Ali Smith

The number of libraries taking part increased. Libraries did not have to commit to buying books for the promotion, but most did. Many libraries bought sets of up to 15 books for reading groups to read.

For a full report on this project see:
www.readingagency.org.uk/reading_partners

poetry for people who don't **read poetry**

Faber working with 30 reading groups

Why don't more readers read poetry? How can libraries get reading groups and users to read poetry?

Libraries have tried this before. Starting poetry reading groups. Pairing novels with poems. Putting poets on with novelists at events. With success.

Recent poetry anthologies have grabbed readers attention. Life. Death. Love. War. The Underground.

If a poetry book or promotion has something special, readers can be encouraged to step outside their safety zone. That's what reader development's business is.

Poetry is Faber's business. They wanted to develop a promotion that would put forward 10 accessible poetry books to open-minded readers.

But which books?

Faber asked 30 fiction reading groups to choose 10 books. Which poetry books are the most accessible? Which books look the most interesting to a person walking past a table of books? Or to a reading group ready to accept a challenge away from prose?

The groups were given 25 poetry collections and anthologies. They chose:

War Poems – Siegfried Sassoon
The Rattle Bag – ed. Seamus Heaney and Ted Hughes
Out of Fashion – ed. Carol Ann Duffy
Old Possums Book of Practical Cats – T S Eliot
Here to Eternity – ed. Andrew Motion
Making Cocoa for Kingsley Amis – Wendy Cope
Emergency Kit – ed. Jo Shapcott and Matthew Sweeney
101 Poems Against the War – ed. Matthew Hollis
Whitsun Weddings – Philip Larkin
Tell Me the Truth About Love – W H Auden

Then Faber created posters, flyers and stickers to support the 10 books – designed specifically for libraries.

They called their promotion *From One Reader to Another*.

Libraries ran the promotion, put up displays in the fiction sections, suggested the books to reading groups for future sessions.

And when most of the books were borrowed in the first three days, the libraries had 100s of other Faber titles – and poetry titles – to keep the promotion alive.

For a full report on this project see:
www.readingagency.org.uk/reading_partners

"

More people visit libraries each year than go to football matches, museums, cinemas, theatres or the country's top ten tourist attractions put together.

Source: Social Trends 35, National Statistics Unit, 2005

"

"
Working with libraries is a joy because they are so enthusiastic about the actual pursuit of reading, whatever form it might take – which is quite easy to lose sight of when we are chasing markets.

Joanna Ellis
Campaign Manager, Faber

"

what to do with **new writers – part one**

Pan working with 48 reading groups to build first novelists

Libraries can help publishers break a new author.

Pan MacMillan put five first-time authors' opening chapters into a sampler. They distributed 1000 to 48 library reading groups. They asked 'Which of these novels would you like to finish reading?'

Each group debated its favourite opening and made a group choice. Pan rewarded them with a set of the book they chose – so that they could finish it.

Then Pan offered some of the libraries author visits; writers visiting libraries near where they lived.

But then the reading groups asked for more. They wanted to read some of the other Pan books. Not just the one they had chosen. They asked their library to include them in the reading list for the next year. Sets were bought.

In all, 750 readers took part. They saw the books on tables in bookshops – the ones they didn't get to finish. Some bought them. Some asked the library to get hold of them. Some told their friends about them.

> For a full report on this project see:
> www.readingagency.org.uk/reading_partners

reading publisher proofs

Random House working with reading groups in the South West

How does a publisher know if a first novel author is going to be a success? How can they build word of mouth for the paperback? Can library reading groups help the publisher to do this – and reinvigorate their own reading at the same time?

Simply Heaven by Serena Mackesy is set in the West Country. Random House worked with the South West's 15 library authorities, reaching over 20 reading groups. They sent out 200 proofs six weeks before publication – with a questionnaire. What did readers think of it? Would they read another book by this author?

The groups read the book with a sense of purpose. They felt they had a responsibility to do so. They read it, not only with their own reading habits in mind, but less judgementally, they said, feeling they were representing the readers of the South West. 'And,' as one librarian said, 'it got their group out of a rut and into trying something new.'

65% of the book's 200 readers finished the book and returned the feedback form to the publisher.

What did Random House do with the results?

Editorial looked at it to see what readers thought of the story.

Marketing used readers' quotes on their selling sheets.

Publicity confirmed it created a buzz about the book in the South West. Word of mouth.

'It is vital to know what real readers think outside the bubble of reviews and the book trade,' said the publisher. 'And all of this helped with the sell in of the paperback.'

word of mouth for emerging writers

Essex Libraries and Random House

Essex Libraries have been at the forefront of reader development for several years. They have 330 reading groups and one of the best library book festivals in the UK.

They got together with Random House to find ways to promote emerging authors, with the intention that each would learn from the other.

How can you build a new author's profile through libraries? How can reading groups help to do that? How can you maintain a reading group's enthusiasm using new and interesting books?

Essex Libraries and Random House chose four books:

> *The Family Tree* – Carole Cadwalladr
> *26a* – Diana Evans
> *The English Dane* – Sarah Bakewell
> *How to Be Lost* – Amanda Eyre Ward

Reading groups read them, discussed them and gave detailed feedback to the publisher.

In March – for the 2006 Essex Book Festival – some of the authors came to speak to reading groups and at larger author events.

As well as knowing that Essex could attract a strong audience to a first-time novelist event, Random House were pleased to bring authors to events where the audience would have read the books. This would make the events for new – and possibly nervous – authors easier, as it would be more an informed discussion of the book than a lecture style event.

The publisher learned from the library how to promote new books in library situations, using local and council PR networks. Also, how reading groups are a great way of building readership for an author.

The library learned from the publisher the techniques of marketing and publicising new authors.

The publisher learned how libraries use displays and recommendation to tempt readers into reading books they'd never normally look at.

Each would bring those skills back into their own work.

> For a full report on this project see:
> www.readingagency.org.uk/reading_partners

access to reading groups **for all**

Orion and Rotherham Libraries

Orion and Rotherham Libraries felt that mainstream reading groups don't always offer full access to disabled readers.

How could they work together to bring disabled readers into all of Rotherham's reading group meetings and represent the make up of the community more realistically?

How could Orion promote their audio book list more imaginatively through libraries?

Together with community groups and council departments that work with disabled people, the library identified disabled readers and offered support that would meet their needs and bring them into the reading group. This gave the publisher an insight into how libraries use other council departments to deliver their services to readers.

Once they recruited readers, the library and publisher made sure that the mainstream reading groups offered an open and inclusive environment, creating reading groups with a breadth of life experience.

> For a full report on this project see:
> www.readingagency.org.uk/reading_partners

" When I read a book I am bursting to speak about it, share my ideas, air my views, unpick my feelings – doing this alone is not satisfactory.

Pontefract Library readers group member

"

more word of mouth –
in derbyshire

Headline and Derbyshire Libraries

Library reading groups contribute to the word of mouth buzz around great books.

Headline worked with reading groups in Derbyshire with a focus on lesser-known literary novels.

The reading groups read several books, commented on them and chose a shortlist to create a library promotion. This gave Headline insight into what libraries' readers like and how they approach books.

Headline created posters and other publicity material to promote the shortlisted books across the region. The publisher and library worked together on the publicity material, each partner learning what the priorities for poster design are in the other sector.

The promotion would run through all Derbyshire's libraries during their 2006 book festival, and Headline would receive coverage in the festival programme.

> For a full report on this project see:
> www.readingagency.org.uk/reading_partners

By socio-economic profile, library users are:

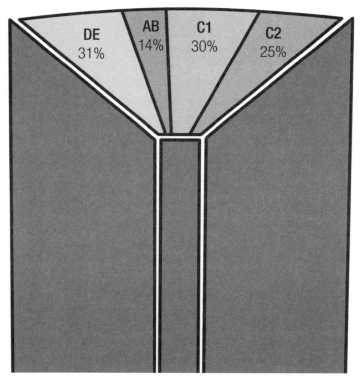

DE
31%

AB
14%

C1
30%

C2
25%

Source: BML, 2001

author events

"I was with an author who was talking to library users after an event. One lady said her husband had really enjoyed hearing the author speak. When the author looked round to see where he was, she explained that his ashes were in the jar she was carrying.

Helen Johnstone
Publicity Manager, HarperCollins Fiction

"

worth **leaving home** for

Nicci Gerard did two author events as part of the Penguin *Readers' Book of the Month* promotion. We asked her how they went.

How did the library events compare to bookshops?

Very well, indeed. There were a lot of people there and it had clearly been well-publicised. The audiences were lovely. There was a sense of being surrounded by people who love books. The events felt relaxed enough to become conversations with the audience rather than remaining formal and one-way.

Was the library well organised?

Yes. Good publicity in advance. Everything laid out and ready. Books to buy and sign were there. Nice introductory speech.

Were you treated well?

Very well indeed. They had gone out of their way to make it feel like a special festive event – something worth leaving home for.

how to **promote an event** –

tips from libraries

- think who might want to come. Where you can reach them. How can you get their attention?

- ask publishers for showcards and other support

- ask publishers for reading group sets of authors' books

- think of a local press story relevant to the author

- ask publishers for a press release template

- get staff to tell all the borrowers about the event

- find local groups and organisations who could be partners in building an audience

- put flyers everywhere – even in council payslips

- exploit libraries' unique contacts with various networks through other council services

how to **promote an event** –

tips from publishers

- use local, regional and national events listings

- use a text or emailing list

- use a postal mailing list

- put posters everywhere

- invite reading groups – library and independents

- work with a bookshop to promote the event

- offer the author to radio and TV, if available

- think of new ways to publicise. Does the event tie into a key date in the calendar?

- talk to the publisher – share ideas, what resources do they have?

how to **run a library author event**

Five tips from library workers

One. Dry run the event with colleagues beforehand to make sure you've covered everything.

Two. Talk to the author about what they want. Run through the format together, so there are no surprises for either of you – for example, do they want to take questions? Think about the author's space. Do they need a lectern, a chair? Have you provided water?

Three. Can you provide any technical support for larger events? A loop system. A microphone and speakers. Can you have the lights on in different ways? What works best for the author?

Four. Know when to stop. Take control of when the event ends. Either set a time and stick to it; or, judge when the audience is sated or the author flagging.

Five. Look after the audience. Make them feel part of something so that they will come to your next event.

how to **run a library author event**

Five tips from publishers

One. When the author arrives (or, even better, you collect them from the station) make them welcome. Put them at ease. They are likely to be more nervous about the event than you.

Two. Be positive at all times. Don't pass on your fears about a low audience, the bad weather, etc.

Three. Make sure the chair or introducer is well briefed and has read the book. It also helps if they lead the questions – to overcome any uncomfortable silences.

Four. Have a good bookstall. Whatever set-up works best for you. Talk to the publisher if you need advice.

Five. Invite the local paper to come and take photos. This adds value to the event and creates ongoing exposure for the author, library event programme and the publisher.

what's the point of events?

1. To introduce new writers to readers
2. To build word of mouth for books and reading
3. To make literature live, like theatre and dance
4. To bring readers together to share the love of books
5. To promote the library and its services
6. To promote a publisher and its list
7. To get press coverage for books or services
8. To get books into hands – through sales or loans
9. To offer entertainment to the community
10. To create a dialogue between the reader and writer

what is a **Readers' Day**?

Libraries invented Readers' Days – a new model to promote reading and authors. Libraries across the country use Readers' Days to bring together hundreds of readers to share tips for great reads. For readers to meet authors, and for authors to meet readers.

The typical format is:

- a panel discussion with three authors talking about their reading as much as their writing
- a choice of reading groups with the authors or other sessions about book covers, reading poetry or other related subjects
- lunch
- a readers fair – stalls to entertain and push readers in the direction of new books
- readers testimonies - three real readers saying what they read and why
- a goody bag for everyone

Bloomsbury ran three Readers' Days with libraries in 2005. Four in 2006.

Readers' Days with a twist.

As well as readers finding out about Bloomsbury authors, the publisher brought editors, jacket designers and marketing people to find out about reading – from readers.

What do readers like? What do readers hate? Do they trust the way books are pitched to them?

Each event sold out to audiences of 100 to 160.

Book sales averaged over £500.

The libraries were efficient.

New readers joined libraries.

The authors were delighted.

So was the publisher. 'Great fun,' Katie Bond, Bloomsbury Publicity Director said. 'And great learning. We've already planned the next one.'

Readers learned about authors and publishing.

Publishers learned about working directly with libraries, and seeing how they use established reading groups, library displays and reading chains to draw more readers into live literature activities and talking about books.

Libraries learned about how publishers market books, their investment in quality promotional material and how they attract press attention.

> For a full report on this project see:
> www.readingagency.org.uk/reading_partners

what to do with **new writers**

HarperCollins touring groups of authors

Reading groups love to discover new writers. The reason they join a group is often to broaden their reading, to challenge their reading.

New writers want to promote themselves. They know they have to.

Libraries want to find new ways of responding to the needs of all readers, putting on activities that people who work all week can still take part in.

HarperCollins wanted to build the profile of new writers.

So, together with four library authorities they set up events across England. These were based on the Readers' Day model but held in the evening.

The publisher produced showcards, a press release template, 400 flyers and 10 posters to support each library's existing publicity techniques.

An average of fifty people attended each event.

After the events the reading groups were enthused and asked to read the authors' books in their next meetings. Libraries bought sets. Neighbouring libraries invited the authors to speak – they'd heard how good it was.

Authors reported enjoying being on tour with other authors, signing lots of books and picking up a few reading tips of their own. 'It was invaluable for me as a first time author,' said one writer.

It was invaluable for HarperCollins too. They wanted to repeat the events. They approached six more libraries. Three in the north of England, three in the south, this time focusing on crime writers.

Libraries offered to have reading groups read backlist books before the event – to help build the audience.

HarperCollins printed quality posters and flyers, advertising the tour. They arranged for the leading crime magazine to promote the event in its pages.

To benefit from each other's expertise, representatives from the six libraries and the publisher got together to share ideas about publicity. How do libraries go about publicising events? How do publishers? What can they learn from each other?

For a full report on this project see:
www.readingagency.org.uk/reading_partners

author events work nationwide

Penguin working in Northern Ireland and Scotland

Some publishers have not carried out as much reader development work in Northern Ireland and Scotland as they'd like to – there is sometimes a hesitancy to support events and reading groups in places that are time consuming and expensive to reach. Unless publishers can be sure it will be a success.

Can the libraries guarantee an audience? Can they run a good event? What track record do they have?

Penguin saw this as a gap in their understanding of readers across the UK. They wanted to work successfully in Northern Ireland and Scotland, as they had in northern English regions such as Yorkshire.

Penguin know that library reading groups offer a successful route in to new areas. So, they partnered with reading groups in Glasgow and Omagh, asking them to read a book by an author from their country.

In Northern Ireland proofs of Irish author Lucy Cauldwell's new novel – *Where They Were Missed* – were read by groups in Omagh.

In Glasgow several groups read 30 hardback copies of Ali Smith's latest novel, *The Accidental*.

Once several groups had read the books, the authors would go and speak to an audience of these readers and other interested library users.

By the end of the project the libraries in Northern Ireland and Scotland would have another success behind them. A track record that other publishers could see for themselves.

Working with reading groups would ensure a strong audience attended the events. It gave the publisher insight into how to promote books in Scotland and Northern Ireland and into how to link authors to readers in their locale.

The libraries learned how to work with a publisher who had experience of working with libraries, building an understand of what publishers' priorities are.

The librarians also met with Penguin to identify which areas of the UK are seen as more of a risk for author events and reading groups. Why they are seen as a risk? What short- and long-term techniques can be set up to help overcome those problems?

For a full report on this project see:
www.readingagency.org.uk/reading_partners

helping libraries and publishers to sell more books

One of the biggest sticking points in partnerships between publishers and libraries has been the sale of books. Libraries want to host more events and promotions with publishers, but do not always have the resources to sell books at them. Publishers and authors want to work more closely with libraries, but are sometimes put off because they do not deliver the sales that make these events worthwhile for them.

The Reading Agency has set out to tackle these issues and make it easier for libraries to sell books. In late 2005 it began a major survey of all UK library authorities, asking them about their levels of book sales, the arrangements they have for those sales, and for ideas to improve them. The results of this research will be published later in 2006.

The report will reveal just how big the library sales market is - something so far unknown. It will show publishers where, when and how libraries sell books, giving them important market knowledge. It will outline how many libraries organise sales of books for themselves, and how many arrange them in partnership with bookshops. The report will also profile some of the library authorities that have built particularly good models for selling books.

Most importantly, The Reading Agency will give libraries practical advice for selling more books. There will be tips on how to plan in advance to make sure audiences of an author event, Readers' Day or similar promotions will have the chance to buy books afterwards. Suppliers and booksellers will also be interested to see how they can improve their service to libraries and work together to maximise sales.

The project will benefit all involved with books. Libraries will be able to provide a better service to their users if they can sell books at their events and promotions. Authors will feel more inclined to take part in events if there is a definite opportunity to sell their books. Publishers will feel more enthusiastic about working with libraries if they can sell their books as well as promote them – and track those sales afterwards. The research will break new ground for publishers and libraries, building on Reading Partners' successful work to bring the two closer together.

> For a full report on this research see:
> www.readingagency.org.uk/reading_partners

using events to enhance a promotion

Faber and Penguin and various libraries

Backing a library book promotion with an event is a great way of broadening its scope, and of reaching new readers.

Once the posters are up, books stickered and flyers out on the table, how do libraries reach the people who don't walk past displays and windows?

Who's going to write a newspaper story about a book promotion?

Who's going to come into the library if they don't normally use it?

Libraries can get news coverage if there's an author coming for an event whose book is part of the promotion. There's the news round-up columns, the events listings. And after the event, a photo of the author standing in front of the promotion.

Events bring in new people. Those who like live arts, but never come to the library. Those who read the paper, but never come to the library.

Penguin backed their *Readers' Book of the Month* promotion with ten events. Authors such as Nicci

Gerard, Elizabeth Buchan and Esther Freud travelled the length and breadth of England.

There was press coverage in most of the towns and cities they visited.

The events raised the profile of the promotion among librarians and library users. And non library users.

Some of the people who attended library live literature events became library users or reading group members. Just from reading about an author visit in the local paper.

Faber's *From One Reader to Another* promotion was about poetry collections and anthologies that are accessible to people who don't normally read poetry.

Some of the poets being promoted were dead. Most of the books were anthologies, so the living poets were less available for events.

Poets have been used by regional libraries in the past to talk about other poets' work.

To get more attention Faber employed a poet – one who knew reader development inside out – to devise an event. John Siddique. An event that would be part poetry reading, part poetry biography, part poetry evangelism.

This poet would go national. Offering an event aimed at reading groups. It would be a throwing down of the gauntlet. A challenge to readers to try poetry for a night. Why you don't need to hate poetry, to fear poetry, or to imagine you'll be bored by poetry. And if you enjoy the event, borrow one of the books and become a poetry reader.

The events would bring in established readers mostly. But to try something new, to broaden their reading.

And to create more interest in the promotion.

For a full report on this project see:
www.readingagency.org.uk/reading_partners

✳

"

Reading Partners has been the key that has unlocked the door between authors and readers – and libraries are in the privileged position of making the introduction.

Carol Ackroyd
Reader Development Officer,
Devon Library & Information Services

"

bringing **young readers** into the library

Lambeth libraries and Time Warner

Lambeth libraries and Time Warner identified young readers – age 16 to 20 – as a joint target. How could they work together to encourage more young people to use the library? And how could Time Warner find out more about this difficult market?

They decided on three events - but not traditional author events that might put young people off. They wanted something more immediately relevant.

One. A film and book night – working with a film and the author of the book of the film, to appeal to both readers and film lovers.

Two. A careers event. Asking the question: What jobs can you get into with reading as a focus? A panel would include: an editor, a journalist and a librarian.

Three. An author event where books would be distributed free beforehand, to encourage young people to read the book, then meet the author.

The project supported a website for the young people to talk online about books, libraries and the issues raised.

> For a full report on this project see:
> www.readingagency.org.uk/reading_partners

local authors – local libraries

Hachette in Scotland, the North West and South West

Authors are normally very willing to speak at libraries. Without a fee – if they are promoting a new book. But who pays for the travel and the accommodation? How do you get the author out from London?

Publishers have limited – often very small – publicity and marketing budgets. The trip from London to the North, Northern Ireland or the South West can be expensive.

Sometimes libraries have a limited budget too. But they do have a venue and a ready made audience of event-goers and reading groups.

And not all authors live in London.

In fact, most don't.

The Reading Partners Author Database lists authors and the region where they live. It's a way of hooking authors up with their local libraries. So they can work together – put on events, visit reading groups, support each other's activities.

Many authors, libraries and publishers know this. And many have found ways to bring the parties together.

Hachette – being Headline, Hodder and Orion – have a lot of regional authors. They're particularly strong in Scotland, the North West and the West Midlands.

They wanted to use the Reading Partners Author Database to plan tours. Two or three authors doing events at libraries near to where they live.

Low travel costs.

No accommodation costs.

Events that would take emerging authors to emerging libraries.

The regional press would support the events because of the local angle.

The authors would build their readership from a solid regional base – helping them get a national foothold.

When authors work with libraries in their region they form a relationship. If a library is running an event and they need an author, they think of who they know can do a good job, someone they can get in touch with easily.

Who do you know who lives nearby?

For a full report on this project see:
www.readingagency.org.uk/reading_partners

──────────── ✳ ────────────

book
promotions

borrowers recommend

It is very difficult to promote emerging authors. Some retailers have been accused of being geared to bestsellers and celebrity books rather than first time authors or backlist.

So how *do* you promote an emerging author?

Libraries and publishers came together in 2005 to create *Borrowers Recommend*. A promotion of books by emerging authors, not chosen by publishers or bookshops, but by library users. Aimed at reading groups and individual readers. Based on the idea of taking a risk, trying something new.

Using the Public Lending Right figures – the total number of books each writer is lending through libraries – *Borrowers Recommend* put forward 21 authors who library users were borrowing in increasing numbers.

The promotion was backed by quality posters, flyers and stickers – with a striking message: these are books that have been Borrowed, Read and Loved.

In the first year *Borrowers Recommend* was a success. Most readers liked it. Most libraries liked it, although some thought they might not at first.

'Unimpressed at first,' said Hull Libraries. However the books have gone great guns and issued very well. We're converted.'

A lot of lessons were learned in year one –
feedback allowing the organisers to fine tune the
promotion for 2006.

The plan is to make *Borrowers Recommend* an
annual event, showcasing the fact that libraries are
catalysts for word of mouth, that readers' choices and
readiness to risk trying new authors in libraries is
creating a place where emerging authors can emerge
even quicker.

In 2006 the promotion will be backed by an
author tour by 10 of the 18 authors taking part, to help
libraries bring in even more new readers.

For a full report on this project see:

---

www.readingagency.org.uk/reading_partners and
www.borrowersrecommend.com

✳

promoting poetry

Faber and Northumbeland Libraries

Many libraries and publishers have a particular focus for their work. Poetry is vital to Faber and also to Northumberland County Council Library Service, home of the Northern Poetry Library.

Northumberland wanted to raise the profile of the Northern Poetry Library both regionally and nationally.

Faber were keen to work with Northumberland – part of a region that has a thriving poetry scene, for readers, writers and live audiences.

To pair up with the Northern Poetry Library, Faber offered an archive of W H Auden's material for a spring exhibition in Morpeth and two major poetry events with Simon Armitage and Don Paterson.

Working together would allow publisher and library authority to develop their events management and publicity techniques together, sharing skills to make sure all activities were a success, coming to understand potential poetry audiences through the partnership, feeding into future projects.

For a full report on this project see:
www.readingagency.org.uk/reading_partners

40% of readers are willing to experiment when borrowing books

20% of readers are willing to experiment when they buy

Book Reading and Public Library Use 2005, BML

new ways of displaying book stock

HarperCollins in the South West and Wales

In 2005 HarperCollins ran a successful partnership with Ottakar's, creating the YouZone, a way to bring readers to books that they might not see in sections of the shop they normally visit.

In 2006 HarperCollins worked with Salisbury and Swansea libraries to pilot similar ideas.

Layout is undergoing huge change in libraries: the pilot would tie in to the search for new thinking.

Salisbury Library worked with HarperCollins to create the YouZone. Working on the idea that people want books about self improvement – physical, spiritual and mental – in the new year, they launched a library YouZone with bespoke posters and banners, a press campaign and partnerships with several local groups and self-help practitioners. Services such as massage, life coaching and meditation were offered. An author of diet books spoke. Book sections were newly badged to direct readers to books and sections they might never have seen under the traditional library Dewey system.

A large window display advertising the launch of the new service showed prominently on the high street.

In Wales readers across the country were asked about fiction. What fiction did they like? Did they think one author was like another? How would they like to see fiction displayed for them to browse?

Hundreds of replies determined a new layout in the fiction sections at Swansea library. New juxtapositions of authors' titles on tables; suggesting: If you like this author, why not try that author.

The library and publisher worked together to model up a space to try out the results of the questionnaire. They created posters and banners to promote it and monitored what worked and what didn't, to move towards future ways of zoning fiction.

A lot was learned from both experiments.

The results fed into the ongoing debate about layout in libraries. More ways to get readers to try books they might not have otherwise seen.

The publisher's support gave the libraries experience of how publishers see their books as an end product, taking on the lessons HarperCollins learned from working with bookshops.

The publishers learned that libraries can be a vibrant place to showcase books and exploring new ways of promoting those books. They also learned that libraries – being networked to each other – can work across a region or country to try out new ideas, new books and new authors. And that libraries have the goodwill of the community and regularly tap into local networks through organisations and other council departments.

> For a full report on this project see:
> www.readingagency.org.uk/reading_partners

reading the male

Pan MacMillan and Stockport Libraries

Pan MacMillan wanted to pair a sales rep with a librarian, to pilot a new model for publishers and libraries working together.

Librarians normally work with publicity or marketing publishers based in London. This project would have the advantage that sales reps are regional: Pan's was based in the North West, the same region as the librarian.

The sales rep's normal job is to sell Pan's books into bookshops and library suppliers in the North West.

The rep and the librarian created a promotion that would appeal to men in their work and leisure places (businesses, pubs, sport centres, etc.). Books to be used would include football, cricket and other sports.

The original idea was to run it in Stockport, but the rest of the North West wanted to take part, so the promotion was rolled out to 22 library authorities.

This appealed to the rep. It would broaden Pan's impact in his sales region.

Sports reading, writing, prizes and a chance to meet sports writers were used as a hook to encourage men to enter a competition and go to their local library. New readers for both libraries and publishers to work with.

The librarian and the rep worked together to design a poster and marketing campaign.

Both had different skills and resources to share. The publisher had access to quality design and print, books and authors. The librarian had access to 500 libraries and readers across a huge area.

The project would tie into a sports reading promotion and Readers Day in the North West in summer 2006. The librarian was delighted to learn about design and marketing from a publisher's standpoint. The publisher was happy to take Pan's books to a market of millions in a very sporting region.

And it would lead to future activities.

'The Pan rep and I will certainly be working on other projects in the future,' said the librarian.

For a full report on this project see:
www.readingagency.org.uk/reading_partners

✳

book acquisition

Mills & Boon and Warwickshire Libraries

Mills & Boon needed to understand how libraries
acquire books – how they could work closer with them
to place the right product in the right library.

A Product Manager publisher attended library
acquisitions meetings to learn how books are bought
and what decisions – stock and budgetary – are made
week to week in libraries. He also talked to librarians
who knew their Mills & Boon readership well – finding
out what demands these readers make on the library.

A librarian attended product, cover and sales
meetings at Mills & Boon. She learned about the
commercial pressures and timing of publications.

They discussed how they work with library
suppliers and how they can get the best out of each
other through that intermediary.

They visited libraries together to share ideas about
how books are bought into libraries and displayed.

> For a full report on this project see:
> www.readingagency.org.uk/reading_partners

libraries

where are **libraries** at?

Libraries are changing. Investment, innovation and partnerships are helping many libraries to become a 21st century reading service to be proud of.

- Online reservations and renewals, supermarket style express book issuing, audio listening posts and library websites use modern technology to deliver a modern service.

- Longer opening hours – including Saturdays and Sundays – and evening events mean those who work traditional hours can use their library more.

- Layout is changing with lower shelving, face-out books, books on tables and comfy seating – as more people are visiting libraries year on year.

- Readers are being encouraged to try different books through reading groups, reading chains, imaginative displays featuring themed books, surprise books, returns trolleys. Also, libraries are backing national promotions like *Richard and Judy*.

the **top 5 reasons** people work for libraries*

1. I love reading

2. I wanted to get books to those who need them

3. I have a passionate belief in the public library system

4. I used libraries as a child – and loved them

5. I am into the idea of free books, information and ideas

* from an email survey of 62 library reader development workers, December 2005

the **top 5 reasons** people work for publishers*

1. I love reading

2. I wanted to work with books

3. It looked like a glamorous career from the outside

4. To work on the national scene

5. To work with authors

* – based on an email survey of 17 publicity publishers, December 2005

working in the regions

To help Reading Partners have a national impact, a network of regional contacts was set up to support communication and planning.

These contacts have found themselves with a new role - representing a wide group of library authorities. In a few regions, identifying this contact was easy, as people were already in place to act as a central point of communication.

One of these, the North West region, has had a co-ordinator post for three years. Jane Mathieson co-ordinates a network of reader development librarians called *Time To Read*. Through this network she is able to develop and support promotions, reading groups and all kinds of author events in the region. Using a website and regular meetings, she brings library reader development experts and enthusiasts together to share ideas and resources and develop skills. They work together on a shared strategy. This allows them to support publisher and other agencies' activities en masse.

In three years, they have run readers' days and promoted dozens of North West writers, many of them published by commercial publishers. They have published a book about their best ideas and activities.

They work in close partnership with national programmes like the BBC's RaW campaign and the Vital Link.

'If a publisher wants to place an activity in the region, all 22 authorities should be equally well-placed in terms of staff skills, motivation and commitment to be able to respond,' said Time To Read Co-ordinator, Jane Mathieson.

The South East now has a regional co-ordinator. All regions have forums where reader development workers come together to share ideas – and to share their enthusiasm for promoting reading.

They welcome publishers' increased support of reader development throughout the UK.

Introduction to the regional set up of libraries

There are 211 library authorities in the UK, all run by local authorities. Each has a library worker with some form of reader development responsibility. Each is part of a regional or home nation reader development network.

Most reader development networks meet up to four times a year to talk about events, promotions and reading group support. The networks feed ideas into the Reading Partners project and help make sure publishers can reach an increasing number of library authorities – and, therefore, readers.

All the regions and their make up are listed in the next 24 pages. Details include the main towns and cities, the reader development forum and a starter contact – the Reading Partners rep – in case publishers don't know library workers in the region that they are interested in.

> The contacts may change after 2006 – an updated list of contacts is available at www.readingagency.org.uk/reading_partners

SCOTLAND

NORTHERN
IRELAND

NORTH
EAST

NORTH
WEST

YORKSHIRE

EAST
MIDLANDS

WEST
MIDLANDS

WALES

EAST

LONDON

SOUTH WEST

SOUTH EAST

Scotland

Main towns and cities
Aberdeen, Dundee, Edinburgh, Glasgow, Inverness

Travel from London
By air to Edinburgh and Glasgow, 1 hour
By rail to Edinburgh and Glasgow, 4 to 5 hours
By road, A1 or M6, 8 hours

Reader Development Network
www.scottishreaders.net
Successful promotions include *Print Options*, *Reading the Festival* and *War in Words*.

Regional contact
Rhona Arthur, Assistant Director, CILIPS/SLIC
Tel: 01698 458888
Email: r.arthur@slainte.org.uk

Scottish library authorities

Aberdeen	Dundee
Aberdeenshire	East Ayrshire
Angus	East Dunbartonshire
Argyll & Bute	East Lothian
Clackmannanshire	East Renfrewshire
Comhairle Nan Eilean Siar	Edinburgh
	Falkirk
Dumfries & Galloway	Fife

Glasgow
Highland
Inverclyde
Midlothian
Moray
North Ayrshire
North Lanarkshire
Orkney
Perth & Kinross

Renfrewshire
Scottish Borders
Shetland
South Ayrshire
South Lanarkshire
Stirling
West Dunbartonshire
West Lothian

Northern Ireland

Main towns and cities
Armagh, Ballymena, Belfast, Coleraine, Enniskillen,
Lisburn, Londonderry, Newry, Omagh

Travel from London
By air, Northern Ireland is served by flights into Belfast
International Airport, Belfast City Airport and City of
Derry Airport. 1 hour.
By sea, coast to coast from Scotland in an hour. High-
speed crossings from England and Wales.

Five Reading Partners representatives, one from each
library board, communicate regularly by email and hold
meetings as necessary.

Regional Contact
Anne McCart
Tel: 0283 7520760
Email: anne.mccart@ni-libraries.net

Northern Ireland's library authorities
Belfast Education and Library Board
North Eastern Education and Library Board
South Eastern Education and Library Board
Southern Education and Library Board
Western Education and Library Board

Wales

Main towns and cities
Cardiff, Newport, Swansea (all South) and Wrexham
(North)

Transport from London
By air via Manchester or Liverpool for North Wales.
For South Wales: Cardiff. For Mid-Wales: Birmingham
or Cardiff.
By rail to North Wales via Chester, Rhyl, Bangor,
Holyhead. London to Chester, 2 hours.
Mainline rail to South Wales via Newport, Cardiff,
Swansea, 2 hours.

By road the M4 is the main route from London to South Wales. 3 hours. Up the M6 to North Wales.

Reader Development Forum

Estyn Allan. Communication network of all 22 library authorities. Three regional groupings work on joint promotions, events and projects. Regional Readers' Days, *Give me a break* promotion and website, book taster sessions. http://www.branching-out.net/welsh_english/welsh/default.asp

Regional Contact

Bethan M. Hughes
Tel: 01824 708207
Email: bethan.hughes@denbighshire.gov.uk

Welsh Library Authorities

Blaenau Gwent	Neath Port Talbot
Bridgend	Newport
Caerphilly	Merthyr Tydfil
Cardiff	Monmouthshire
Carmarthenshire	Pembrokeshire
Ceredigion	Powys
Conwy	Rhondda Cynon Taff
Denbighshire	Swansea
Flintshire	Torfaen
Gwynedd	Vale of Glamorgan
Isle of Anglesey	Wrexham

North East England

Where is it?
250 miles north of London

Main towns and cities
Durham, Gateshead, Middlesbrough, Newcastle, Stockton, Sunderland

Travel from London
By air from Stanstead to Newcastle, 45 minutes
By rail from London direct to Darlington, Durham and Newcastle, 3 hours
By car, A1 north, 4 hours

Reader Development Network
Reading North, funded by Arts Council England North East, meet bi-monthly. They have run an annual regional Readers' Day in September since 2001.

Regional contact
Joanne Parkinson
Tel: 0191 219 3448
Email: joanne.parkinson@sunderland.gov.uk

North East library authorities:

Darlington	Hartlepool
Durham	Middlesbrough
Gateshead	Newcastle

North Tyneside
Northumberland
Redcar & Cleveland

South Tyneside
Stockton
Sunderland

North West England

Where is it?

150 miles north of London

Main towns and cities:

Carlisle, Manchester, Lancaster, Liverpool, Preston, Blackburn

Travel from London

By air to Manchester and Liverpool, under an hour

By rail, 2 hours and 15 minutes

By road, M6 from three hours.

Reader Development Network

Time to Read has a business plan and regional strategy, works on cross-regional projects and meets every eight weeks. It employs a full time co-ordinator, based in Manchester. It is funded by the 22 North West Library authorities, MLA NW and ACE NW. The website address is www.time-to-read.co.uk

Regional contact

Jane Mathieson

Tel: 0161 236 4451

Email: nwreader.libraries@manchester.gov.uk

North West library authorities

Blackburn	Oldham
Blackpool	Rochdale
Bolton	Salford
Bury	Sefton
Cheshire	St Helens
Cumbria	Stockport
Halton	Tameside
Knowsley	Trafford
Lancashire	Warrington
Liverpool	Wigan
Manchester	Wirral

Yorkshire

Where is it?

160 miles north of London

Main cities

Leeds, Bradford, Hull, Sheffield, York

Travel from London

By air to Leeds/Bradford airport, 1 hour

By rail direct to Leeds, York, Doncaster, 2 hours

By road, A1 and M1, 3 hours

Reader Development Network

Read Yorkshire meets three times a year. In 2002 they delivered the UK's first 12 Readers' Days as a consortium. Funded by Arts Council England, Yorkshire and the 15 library authorities. Currently working on a regional strategy document and plans for future years.

Regional Contact

Bernard Murphy

Tel: 01422 392630

Email: bernard.murphy@calderdale.gov.uk

Yorkshire's library authorities:

Barnsley	Leeds
Bradford	North East Lincolnshire
Calderdale (Halifax)	North Yorkshire
Doncaster	Rotherham
East Lincolnshire	Sheffield
East Yorkshire	Wakefield
Hull	York
Kirklees (Huddersfield)	

West Midlands

Where is it?

70 miles north west of London

Main cities

Birmingham, Coventry, Stoke on Trent, Walsall, Wolverhampton

Travel from London

By rail from Euston, less than 2 hours
By road, M40, 2 hours

Reader Development Network

A regional forum was reformed in early 2006. Reader development workers meet regularly.

Regional contact

Nicola Thomas
Tel: 0121 704 6965
Email: nicolathomas@solihull.gov.uk

West Midlands library authorities

Birmingham	Staffordshire
Coventry	Stoke on Trent
Dudley	Telford and Wrekin
Herefordshire	Walsall
Sandwell	Warwickshire
Shropshire	Wolverhampton
Solihull	Worcestershire

East Midlands

Where is it?
70 miles north of London

Main towns and cities
Chesterfield, Derby, Leicester, Lincoln, Northampton, Nottingham

Travel from London
By air to Nottingham East Midlands airport, 1 hour
By rail, 1 to 2 hours
By road (M1) one and a half to two hours

Reader Development Network
EMRALD, East Midlands' public libraries, working together to promote books and reading. EMRALD created a website www.whatareyouuptotonight.com. Funded by the library authorities with additional project support from Arts Council England and EMMLAC.

Regional contact
Lynn Hodgkins
Tel: 01773 835064
Email: lynn.hodgkins@derbyshire.gov.uk

East Midlands library authorities

Derby

Derbyshire

Leicester

Leicestershire

Lincolnshire

Northamptonshire

Nottingham

Nottinghamshire

Northamptonshire

Rutland

East England

Where is it?

From Norfolk down to Essex and inland to
Cambridgeshire

Main towns and cities

Bedford, Cambridge, Chelmsford, Colchester, Ipswich,
Luton, Norwich, Peterborough, Southend, St Albans,
Thurrock, Watford

Travel from London

By rail, within 2 hours

By road, up M11, A1, A12 and M25, 30 minutes to 3
hours

Reader Development Network

Read East is a network of reader development leads to
build and champion good practice and expand regional
opportunities for the enjoyment of reading. Meets four

times a year. Funded by each authority and originally by the Society of Chief Librarians.

Contact
Sylvia Voaden
Tel: 01353 616168
sylvia.voaden@cambridgeshire.gov.uk
Lorna Payne
lorna.payne@norfolk.gov.uk

East England library authorities

Bedfordshire	Norfolk
Cambridgeshire	Peterborough
Essex	Southend
Hertfordshire	Suffolk
Luton	Thurrock

South West England

Where is it?
150 to 300 miles west of London

Main towns and cities
Bournemouth, Bristol, Exeter, Gloucester, Plymouth

Travel from London
By air to Bristol, Newquay, Exeter, Bournemouth and Plymouth – under an hour

By rail around two hours
By car, M4 west, linking to the M5, from 3 hours

Reader Development Network
Read South West is a partnership between 15 library authorities and the Arts Council. Currently seeking to formalise its role with the adoption of a revised strategy and action plan. Meets three times a year. Funded by each authority and lottery/Arts Council England for projects.

Regional Contact
Carol Ackroyd
Tel: 01392 385919
Email: carol.ackroyd@devon.gov.uk

South West library authorities

Bath & N E Somerset	Poole
Bournemouth	Plymouth
Bristol	Somerset
Cornwall	South Gloucestershire
Devon	Swindon
Dorset	Torbay
Gloucestershire	Wiltshire
North Somerset	

South East England

Where is it?
Surrounding London from the south coast north to
Milton Keynes, east to Kent and west to Hampshire

Main cities:
Basingstoke, Brighton and Hove, Guilford, Milton
Keynes, Oxford, Portsmouth, Rochester, Southampton

Travel from London
By rail, services out of all main London train stations
By road, key M and A roads, up to 2 hours

Reader Development Network
South East Reading Development Partnership meets
regularly, co-ordinated by a full time worker since July
2005. It is funded by SEMLAC, Arts Council England,
South East and the Society of Chief Librarians. Recent
successes include Readers' Day and *One City One Read*
promotions. A regional strategy is currently being
developed.

Regional Contact:
Ruth Wells, SEMLAC
Tel: 07899 987810
Email: ruthw@semlac.org.uk

South East England library authorities

Bracknell Forest

Brighton and Hove

Buckinghamshire

East Sussex

Hampshire

Isle of Wight

Kent

Medway

Milton Keynes

Oxfordshire

Portsmouth

Reading

Slough

Southampton

Surrey

West Berkshire

West Sussex

Windsor and Maidenhead

Wokingham

London

Reader Development Network

The London Libraries Recommend promotional steering group, coordinated by the London Libraries Development Agency (LLDA). They meet monthly and produce two London-wide book promotions a year. www.londonlibraries.org. Funded in 2005–2006 by the Arts Council and ALM London.

Regional contact

Rupert Colley

Tel: 020 8379 8393

Email: rupert.colley@enfield.gov.uk

London Libraries Development Agency
Fiona O'Brien
Tel: 020 7641 5233
Email: fiona.obrien@llda.org.uk

London's Library Authorities
City of Westminster
City of London
London Borough of Barking and Dagenham
London Borough of Barnet
London Borough of Bexley
London Borough of Brent
London Borough of Bromley
London Borough of Camden
London Borough of Croydon
London Borough of Ealing
London Borough of Enfield
London Borough of Greenwich
London Borough of Hackney
London Borough of Hammersmith and Fulham
London Borough of Harringey
London Borough of Harrow
London Borough of Havering
London Borough of Hillingdon
London Borough of Hounslow
London Borough of Islington
London Borough of Lambeth
London Borough of Lewisham

London Borough of Merton
London Borough of Newham
London Borough of Redbridge
London Borough of Richmond upon Thames
London Borough of Southwark
London Borough of Sutton
London Borough of Tower Hamlets
London Borough of Waltham Forest
London Borough of Wandsworth
Royal Borough of Kensington and Chelsea
Royal Borough of Kingston upon Thames

Others Parts of the UK

Guernsey Libraries
Edward Jewell
ejewell@library.gg

States of Jersey
Judith Baker
j.baker2@gov.je

Isle of Man
Pamela Hand
oncan.library@onchan.org.im

"

People working in libraries...
seem to me to represent the
frontline of readers in a way
that bookshops do not; they
understand readers' loves,
hates, boredoms, passions
and quirks in an exceptional
way.

Kath Viner
The *Guardian*

"

ten **top websites** among library workers*

www.orangeprize.co.uk

www.branchingout.net/talkingshop

www.readingagency.org.uk

www.bookcrossing.com

www.whichbook.net

www.everybodysreading.com

www.readinggroups.co.uk

www.randomhouse.co.uk/readersgroup

www.penguin.co.uk/readers

www.time-to-read.co.uk

* from an email survey of 62 library reader development workers, December 2005

20% of readers trust a book recommendation from
library staff

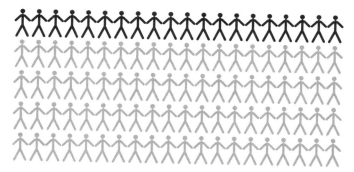

5% of readers trust a book recommendation from a
bookseller

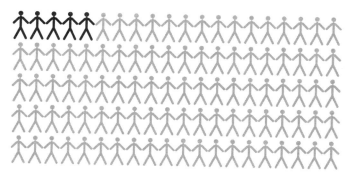

"

As a child growing up in the middle of nowhere, the library van was my lifeline. Now as a first-time author the support of libraries countrywide has been a lifeline. The Readers' Days, the library book groups and tours I have been part of were simply invaluable.

Tiffany Murray
Author of *Happy Accidents*

"

publishers

"

The enthusiasm from libraries for reading is so refreshing and genuine – a great antidote to the world of media which can often be preoccupied with the next topical or celebrity driven title rather than simply by great writing.

Helen Johnstone
Publicity Manager, HarperCollins Fiction

"

publisher bug bears with libraries*

'They don't understand that publishers have to justify every penny spent to their bosses.'

'Bureaucracy. Red tape.'

'An obsession with hierarchy.'

'Focus and budget can be about politically correct issues, rather than books.'

'Libraries who ring up saying they want an author, any author.'

'Unrealistic expectations of authors' time.'

* from an email survey of 17 publicity publishers, December 2005

library bug bears with publishers*

- 'They never return your calls.'

- 'You always have to chase them up.'

- 'Short deadlines for promotions and activities.'

- 'Saying they want a guaranteed audience.'

- 'Publishers seem to have two speeds – "dead slow" and "we need to know yesterday" with nothing in between.'

* based on an email survey of 62 library reader development workers, December 2005

publishers **need a** library specialist

Random House's Rebecca Ash spent a lot of 2005 working with libraries. She has become something of a libraries specialist, one of several publishers with a similar role.

Rebecca worked on the Vintage Future Classics promotion for Random House

Her role is vital to libraries, in that she acts as an advocate within Random House, talking to publicity and marketing departments about how publishers can benefit from library promotions, events and reading group work.

'Departments are much more receptive to libraries now,' Rebecca says. 'Since Vintage Future Classics the profile of libraries and who we work with has improved.'

Rebecca circulates ideas and database information to her colleagues to help this happen.

'But there is still a long way to go,' she adds.

Other publishers with library specialists in this area include Pan MacMillan, HarperCollins and Penguin.

how to pitch to publishers – advice for libraries

It can be quite intimidating cold-calling a publisher, requesting an author for an event. One trick is to put yourself in the position of the publicist.

You look after 20 authors. The commercial pressures are huge. Your budget is surprisingly small – unless it's a big name author. You want creative ways to get your author's name about. You want to be sure it'll be worth the investment of time and money. Otherwise you'll look like you can't do your job.

As a librarian, you need to tell the publicist what you are going to do to make sure yours is a going to be a worthwhile event. What are you going to do to make sure that happens? What information can you give them?

A senior publicist at HarperCollins suggests you consider and tell them about the following to improve your chances of them providing an author for your event. This doesn't mean you need all this information before you make a pitch. But if you can provide it as the event planning develops it will go a long way to making the event happen – and should lead to a good library – publisher relationship.

- Is the author going to be promoting a new book?
- Does the author live within range of your venue?
- Can you show you have a good record of events?
- Can you show you have planned the event?
- Where and when will the event be held?
- Who is your target audience? And how many?
- Will there be other speakers? And, if so, who?
- Will the event be chaired? Who by?
- Who is selling the books? How many do you expect to sell?
- Is the event ticketed? How much?
- How will you promote the event?
- What promotional support do you need from the publisher?
- How long do you want the author to speak for?
- What format will the event take: panel, debate, workshop, reading, interview, reading group, signing?
- Who is the library contact for the author?
- Who will meet, greet and transport them?
- Is there a fee or travel expenses?
- Will you provide a meal before or after the event?
- Do you have a microphone or audio loop system and have you alerted the author?
- Do you have overnight accommodation in mind?
- How far from London are you? How do you get to your library from London?

- Are you approaching the publisher alone or with one or more other library authorities?
- Is your venue on the Reading Partners venue database?

This should give you an idea of how some publishers are thinking. It lays out what they want – especially for larger scale events.

More and more publishers and libraries are working together to define what needs doing by both sides to make an event a success.

Before recent author tours to libraries, meetings with publishers in libraries have helped both parties plan publicity together.

> The Reading Agency website has a form that you can fill in and send to publishers with all this information. Available at
> www.readingagency.org.uk/reading_partners

directory of reading partners **publishers**

It can be a nightmare finding the right person to talk to at a publisher. We suggest two ways.

One. If you know the publisher and imprint of the book or author you are interested in visit www.publisherspublicitycircle.co.uk, which lists hundreds of publicists by imprint.

Two. Telephone the switchboard of the publisher and ask to be put through to the right person (e.g. 'the publicist for Will Self' or 'the person in the marketing department dealing with sports books.')

Here are the switchboard numbers for the Reading Partners publishers, with a list of imprints they house:

Bloomsbury
020 7494 2111
www.bloomsburymagazine.com

Faber
020 7465 0045
www.faber.co.uk

Harlequin Mills & Boon

020 8288 2800

www.eharlequin.co.uk and www.millsandboon.co.uk

Mills & Boon, Mira, Silhouette

HarperCollins

020 8741 7070

www.harpercollins.co.uk

HarperCollins, Collins Crime, Voyager, Harper Press,
Fourth Estate, Harper Perennial

Hodder Headline

020 7873 6000

www.hodderheadline.co.uk

Coronet, Flame, Headline, Headline Review, Hodder,
New English Library, Sceptre

Orion

020 7240 3444

www.orionbooks.co.uk

Cassell, Everyman, Gollancz, Orion, Phoenix Press,
Weidenfeld & Nicolson

Pan MacMillan

020 7833 4000

www.macmillan.co.uk

Boxtree, Campbell Books, MacMillan, Pan, Picador,
Sidgwick & Jackson

Penguin

020 7010 3000

www.penguin.co.uk

Allen Lane, Dorling Kindersley, Frederick Warne, Hamish Hamilton, Ladybird, Michael Joseph, Penguin, Puffin, Ventura, Viking

Random House

020 7840 8400

www.randomhouse.co.uk

Arrow, Bodley Head, Century, Chatto & Windus, Corgi, David Fickling, Doubleday, Ebury, Fodors, Harvill Secker, Hutchinson, Jonathan Cape, Pimlico, Red Fox, Rider, Vermillion, Vintage, William Heinemann, Yellow Jersey Press

Time Warner

020 7911 8000

www.timewarnerbooks.co.uk

Abacus, Atom, Little Brown, Orbit, Time Warner, Virago, X Libris

Transworld

020 8579 2652

www.booksattransworld.co.uk

Bantam, Black Swan, Corgi, Doubleday, Eden, Expert Books

general information

Reading Partners has created four databases to help libraries talk to the right publishers and publishers to the right libraries.

Database of Library Event Venues

The venue database details hundreds of library venues that hold audiences of between 30 and 1500. The database was designed by publishers. It includes lists of audience capacity, publicity, local bookseller, reading group and mailing list information, amongst much more.

Available in electronic or paper format for all publishers who are part of Reading Partners. Updated three times a year. Contact tom.palmer@readingagency.org.uk

Database of Where Authors Live

To bring authors together with libraries in their region, publishers have supplied a list of authors who want to work in libraries, where they live, what they've written and how to get in touch with them.

Available in 2006 at www.readingagency.org.uk/reading_partners

Rolling Calendar

For libraries. A huge month-by-month list of authors promoting books, proofs available, posters available, publisher promotions and general dates in the calendar. Goes six to twelve months into the future.

Available at www.readingagency.org.uk/reading_partners

What's Planned in Libraries

A database of what festivals, major events, Readers' Days, anniversaries, library openings and other activities are planned in all the UK's libraries. For publishers to tie in with existing activities.

Available at www.readingagency.org.uk/reading_partners

———————— ✳ ————————

the **library-publisher-supplier** code of practice

Library users deserve access to new and promoted titles that's as fast as it is for bookshop users.

Amanda Ridout
Managing Director, HarperCollins General Books

A new Code of Practice for library supply aims to improve the speed of supply of new and promoted titles to libraries.

The Code came out of a meeting between publishers, librarians and library suppliers and sowed the seeds for increased networking and communication between all three parties.

Publishers agreed to put libraries on the first release date for new publications.

Library suppliers and the Reading Agency work together to support libraries in making the most of promotions – by making sure books are in libraries the day a promotion starts.

The code suggests a timescale for publishers to use to work backwards and make sure libraries get the books on time.

It is reproduced in full on the next three pages.

code of practice for **book supply to libraries**

Publication Information

1. **Publishers** to provide accurate pre-publication information about authors and titles for new publications and books featuring in promotions to Book Data Services with updates as they become available

2. **Publishers** to supply a publication date for each title on their advance information to library suppliers and supply date changes as they occur

3. **Publishers** to provide library suppliers with a cut-off day for orders for new publications and books featuring in promotions. This date should be 3–4 months before publication date where possible

4. **Library suppliers** to advise libraries of new publications and books featuring in promotions prior to publication and give the publication dates and cut-off dates for orders

Supply

5. **Libraries** to place orders by cut-off date indicated by library suppliers

6. **Library Suppliers** to estimate library orders for new publications and books featuring in promotions immediately based on knowledge of orders for similar titles rather than waiting for orders from libraries

7. **Publishers** to ensure library suppliers are on the first UK release for all lead titles and prize winners, provided that library suppliers conform to regulations on embargo and supply

8. **Library suppliers** to ensure new publications and books featuring in promotions are delivered to libraries on publication date/embargo date

9. **TRA** to manage co-ordination of book supply for national promotions (where possible) on behalf of the libraries In England, Wales and Northern Ireland and provide information to libraries and library suppliers at the earliest possible release date

10. **Library suppliers** to label boxes of new publications and books featuring in promotions clearly on the outside to ensure that they are easily identifiable from other library deliveries

11. **Libraries** to unpack books and ensure they are available in libraries on publication date or within three working days - depending on internal transport.

Point of Sale

12. **TRA** to manage co-ordination of point of sale for national promotions (where possible) on behalf of the libraries in England, Wales and Northern Ireland and provide information to libraries and library suppliers at the earliest possible release date

13. **Publishers** to supply any relevant promotional materials in time to be dispatched with the books i.e. for delivery on date of publication/ embargo date

14. **Library suppliers** to pack any promotional materials made available to support books so that they arrive undamaged in libraries, and the parcel contents are clearly labelled

15. **Libraries** to unpack and display promotional material on publication date or within three working days of publication date depending on internal transport systems

acknowledgements

This book would not have been possible without the input of about 300 library workers from 211 library authorities, 150 publishers from 9 publishing houses and 3000 readers from over 150 reading groups. The Reading Agency is very grateful to them all – for showing that working together, publishers, libraries and readers can create new ways of bringing more books to more readers.

Reading Partners have received an investment from Arts & Business New Partners to develop their creative partnership. Arts & Business New Partners is funded by Arts Council England and the Department for Culture, Media and Sport. Their support has meant libraries and publishers have been able to share new skills and understanding.

Other funders of projects are MLA (from the *Framework for the Future Action Plan*) and the publishers Bloomsbury Publishing plc, Faber & Faber Ltd, Hachette Livre, Harlequin Mills & Boon Ltd, HarperCollins Publishers Ltd, Pan MacMillan, Penguin Group (UK), The Random House Group Ltd and Time Warner Books UK. Also Arts Council, Scotland.

Of the hundreds mentioned above, we'd like to especially thank the following: Carol Ackroyd, Rhona Arthur, Rebecca Ash, Jessica Axe, Nigel Baines, Andrew Belshaw, Kevin Blackwell, Katie Bond, Gerry Burns, Alison Byrne, Julie Clement, Rupert Colley, Nicole de Weirdt, Anne-Marie Dossett, Joanna Ellis, Laurence Festal, Kate Fox, Minna Fry, Rosie Gailer, Patrick Gale, Nikki Gerard, Elaine Glenwright, Marie Gray, Rebecca Gray, Mary Greenshields, Pat Hallam, Clare Harington, Ruth Harrison, Charlotte Hawes, Britta Heyworth, Angela Hicken, Julie Hird, Lynn Hodgkins, Tom Holman, Susan Holmes, Paul Howarth, Bethan Hughes, Helen Johnstone, Rosalie MacFarlane, Bernie Macmanamon, Anne McCart, Fiona McIntosh, Alison McKellar, Angela McMahon, Katherine Muller, Bernard Murphy, Noel Murphy, Tiffany Murray, Deidre Nugent, Joanne Parkinson, Joanna Prior, Oliver Rhodes, Amanda Ridout, Alison Shakspeare, Susanna Skinner, Clare Somerville, Andrew Stevens, Louisa Symington, Nicola Thomas, Philip Tomes, Helena Towers, Anne Tucker and Sylvia Voaden.

Thanks are due in particular to Katie Bond of Bloomsbury who gave superb editorial support, as did the Reading Partners regional reps, Jane Mathieson (North West) and Ruth Wells (South East). Also to Lee Motley, Louise Edwards and Terence Caven at

HarperCollins for designing the book and Tiina Wastie from Penguin for its production. Your work on this book is very much appreciated!

The author would like to thank Rebecca and Iris Palmer for their round-the-clock patience and encouragement.

**Tom Palmer, Penny Shapland
and Miranda McKearney**

picture credits